Why *Daily Handwriting Practice?*

The premise behind *Daily Handwriting Practice* is simple and straightforward—frequent, focused practice of a skill leads to mastery and retention of that skill.

What's in *Daily Handwriting Practice?*

- The book is divided into 36 weekly sections. On Monday through Thursday students complete half pages to practice writing letters, words, and sentences. Friday's practice is a full page.

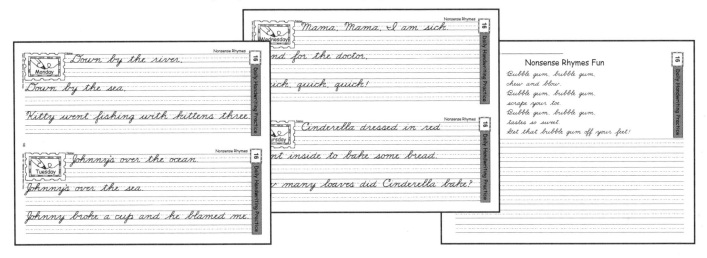

- A full-page chart showing proper letter formation is included.

- *Daily Handwriting Practice* is more than handwriting. While completing the handwriting exercises, students learn about a variety of curriculum topics:

The Alphabet	Unusual Animals
Capital Letters	Owls Are Amazing Hunters
Months of the Year	Whales
Days of the Week	The Water Cycle
Geography Facts	Using Good Verbs
Inventors	Figures of Speech
The Seven Continents	Colors and Alliteration
The Weather	Learning About Beavers
Our Presidents	Simple Machines
Games Around the World	Famous Quotations
Native American Tribes	Sports Around the World
Unusual Plants	Candy Around the World
Prefixes and Suffixes	Learning About Kenya
Rhyming Words	Writing About Math
Rivers of the World	Alphabets Around the World
Nonsense Rhymes	

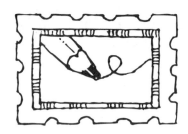

Letter Formation Chart
Traditional Cursive

Aa *Bb* *Cc* *Dd*

Ee *Ff* *Gg* *Hh*

Ii *Jj* *Kk* *Ll*

Mm *Nn* *Oo* *Pp*

Qq *Rr* *Ss* *Tt*

Uu *Vv* *Ww* *Xx*

Yy *Zz*

     Daily Handwriting Practice • EMC 791

Name:

Monday

a a a   b b b

c c c   d d d

e e e   f f f

cat   dat   trad

face   ace   tread

fee   traa   deed

Name:

Tuesday

g g g   h h h

i i i   j j j

k k k   l l l

kid   bid   bit

leg   hill   jat

dig   big   cake

3

The Alphabet

Name:

Wednesday

m m m m

o o o

g g g

p p p

n n n

moon   race

roam   drop

bran   pail

poem

mane

drape

The Alphabet

Name:

Thursday

s s s

t t t

u u u

v v v

w w w

x x x

y y y

z z z

amazing

windows

years

quiet

4

Name: _____

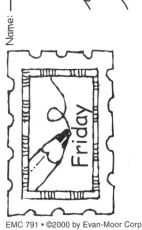

Friday

In Just

when the world is puddle-wonderful

the queer old balloonman whistles

far and wee

and betty and isbel come dancing

from hop-scotch and jump-rope and

it's spring

e.e. cummings

e.e. cummings is a poet who uses very few capital letters.
Practice your lowercase letters by copying this stanza from his poem.

Sign your name like e.e. cummings. Use your first two initials and your last name with no capitals.

Capital Letters

Name:

Monday

A B C D E
F G H I J

Bob
Dastri
Fran
Hoa

Amber
Carlos
Eddie
Gunter

Capital Letters

Name:

Tuesday

K L M N O
P Q R

Kanika
Maria
Olga
Quon

Jamal
Lana
Namid
Raul
Paul

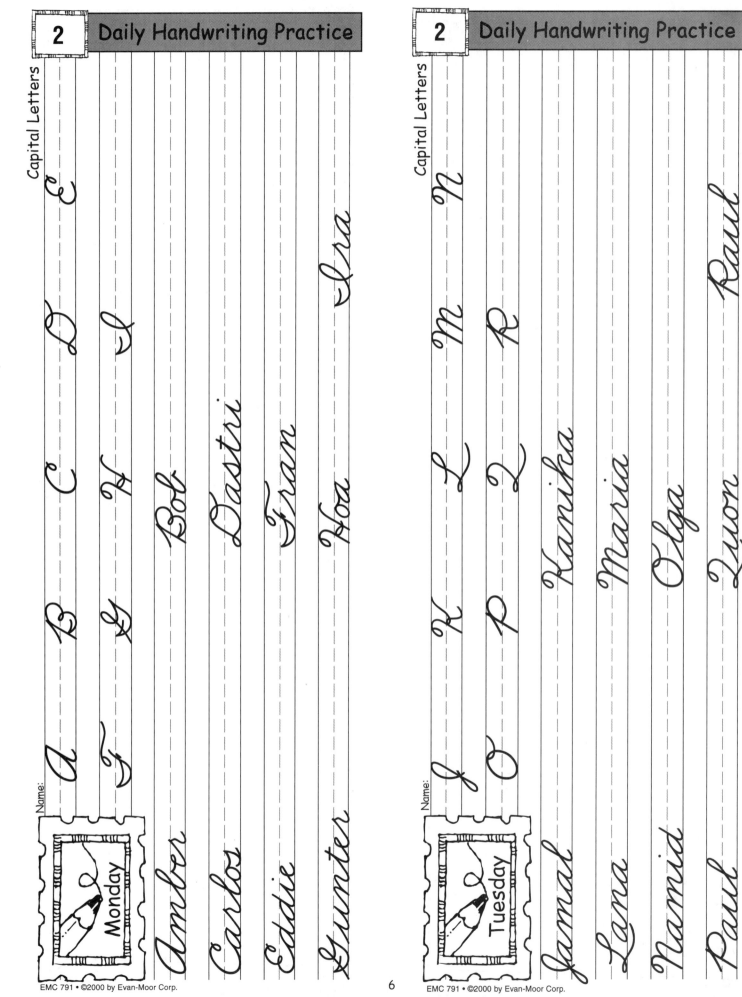

Capital Letters

Name:

Wednesday

A F U V

W X Y Z

Tima

Victor

Xavier

Zeke

Scott

Usef

Walker

Yasmin

Capital Letters

Name:

Thursday

Aa Bb Cc Dd

Ee Ff Gg Hh

Ii Jj Kk Ll

Mm Nn Oo Pp

Qq Rr Ss Tt

Uu Vv Ww Xx Yy Zz

Name: _____

Friday

A Dialogue

Student: A, B, C, D, Eeee! A bee!

Teacher: No. A, B, C, D, E, F

Student: A, B, C, D, E, F, Gee, a bee!

Teacher: No. No. No.

Student: A bee!

Teacher: That's better. A, B, C...

Copy the letters and the words written in cursive.

Months of the Year

Name:

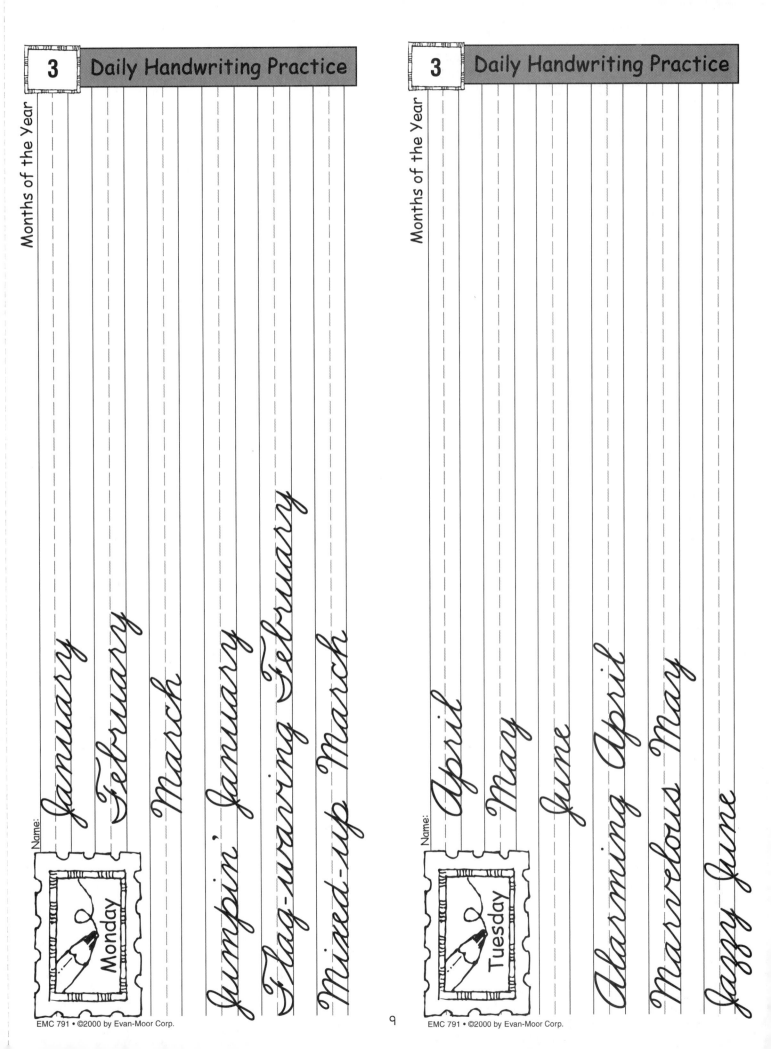

Monday

January

February

March

Jumpin' January

Flag-waving February

Mixed-up March

Months of the Year

Name:

Tuesday

April

May

June

Alarming April

Marvelous May

Jazzy June

Months of the Year

Name:

Wednesday

July

August

September

Jolly July

Ambitious August

Spirited September

Months of the Year

Name:

Thursday

October

November

December

Orderly October

Next-to-last November

Dazzling December

Name: _____

Friday

Months of the Year

January	February	March
April	May	June
July	August	September
October	November	December

Write the months in alphabetical order.

Days of the Week

Name:

Monday

Tuesday

Monday mornings make me merry.

Tuesday twilight turns into tomorrow.

12

Days of the Week

Name:

Tuesday

Wednesday

Thursday

Wild Wednesday winds whistle.

Thursday tornadoes turn treacherous.

Days of the Week

Name:

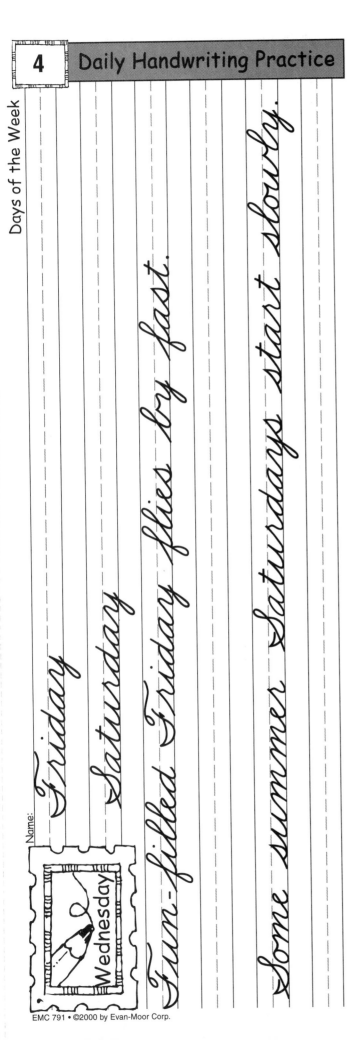

Friday

Saturday

Fun-filled Friday flies by fast.

Some summer Saturdays start slowly.

Days of the Week

Name:

Sunday

swim

shower

Sunday's sun swims into showers.

Soon the showers slip back to sun.

Days of the Week

Name: _____

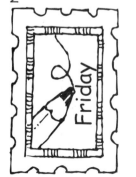

Friday

Monday's child is fair of face,
Tuesday's child is full of grace.
Wednesday's child is full of woe,
Thursday's child has far to go,
Friday's child is loving and giving,
Saturday's child works for a living;
But the child that's born on Sunday
Is blithe and bonny, good and gay.

Copy this Mother Goose rhyme.

Name:

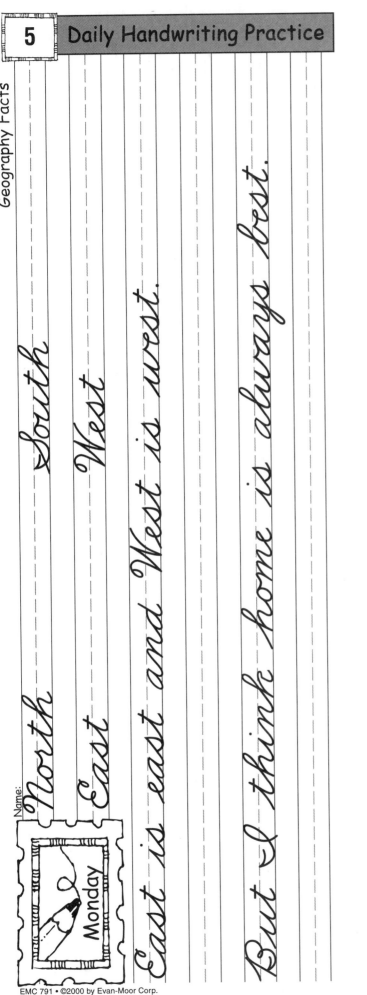

Monday

North   South

East   West

East is east and West is west.

But I think home is always best.

Name:

Tuesday

compass rose

legend

The compass rose shows directions.

The legend of a map is a key.

Name:

Wednesday

equator

prime meridian

These are imaginary lines on a map.

They help people describe locations.

Name:

Thursday

North Pole

South Pole

The North Pole is at the top of a globe.

The South Pole is at the bottom.

Geography Facts

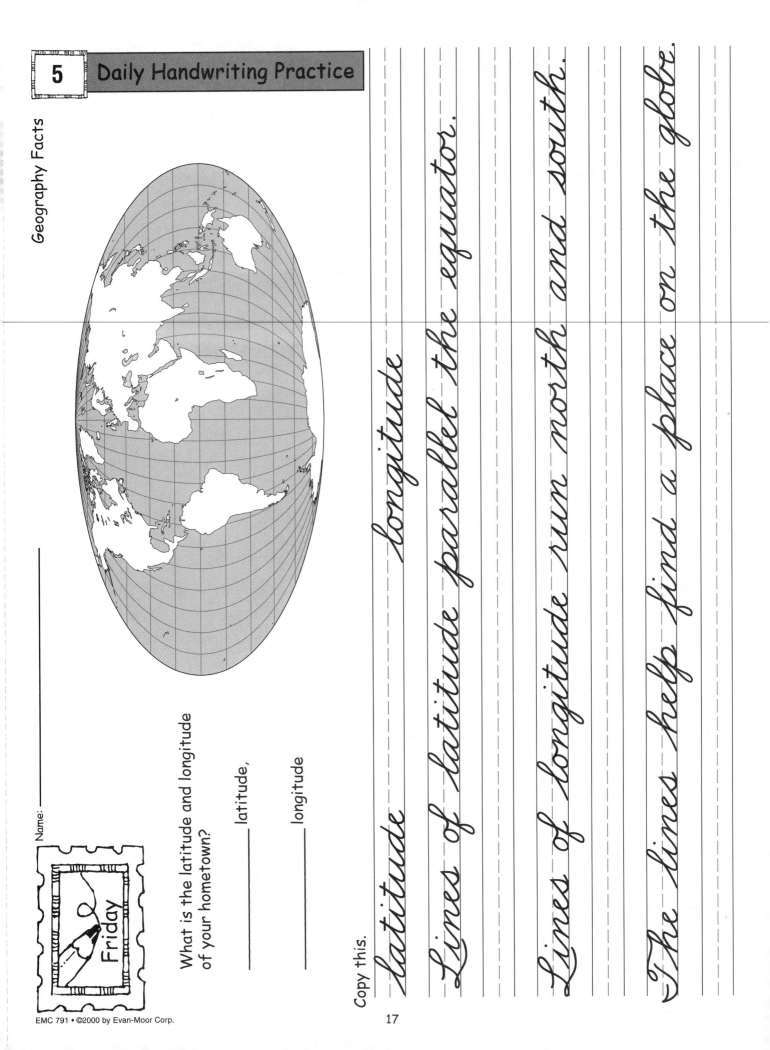

Name: _____

Friday

What is the latitude and longitude of your hometown?

_____ latitude,

_____ longitude

Copy this.

latitude

longitude

Lines of latitude parallel the equator.

Lines of longitude run north and south.

The lines help find a place on the globe.

Inventors

Name:

Monday

telephones

A. G. Bell

Mr. Bell patented the telephone in 1876.

Today there are more than 425 million.

18

(R. J. Anderson patented the idea of a washing machine with wooden tubs.)

Inventors

Name:

Tuesday

washing machines

R. J. Anderson

People used to wash clothes by hand.

Then washing machines were invented.

Name:

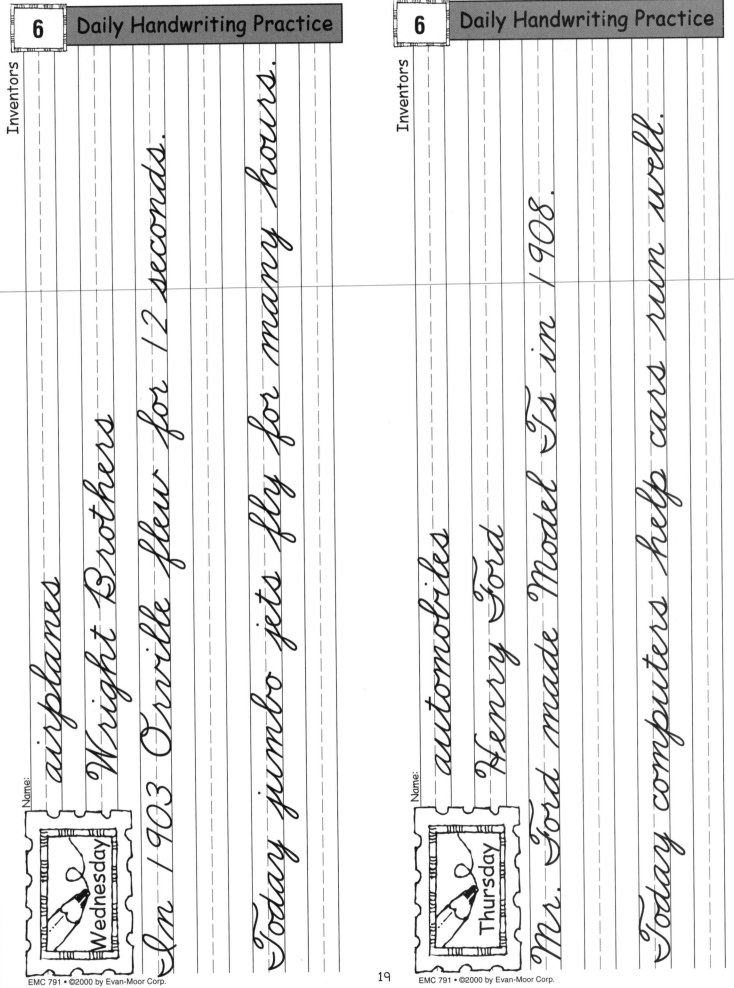

Wednesday

airplanes

Wright Brothers

In 1903 Orville flew for 12 seconds.

Today jumbo jets fly for many hours.

Name:

Thursday

automobiles

Henry Ford

Mr. Ford made Model T's in 1908.

Today computers help cars run well.

Name: _____

Friday

Famous Inventors

Jacques Cousteau	SCUBA
Thomas Edison	light bulb
Benjamin Franklin	bifocals
Galileo Galilei	telescope
Louis Pasteur	pasteurization
George Westinghouse	air brakes
Steve Wozniak	personal computer

Copy the names of these famous inventors.

Jacques Cousteau

Thomas Edison

Benjamin Franklin

Galileo Galilei

Louis Pasteur

George Westinghouse

Steve Wozniak

Name:

Monday

continent

landmass

A continent is a large landmass.

The Earth has seven major continents.

Name:

Tuesday

North America

South America

is north of the equator.

is south of the equator.

The Seven Continents

Name:

Wednesday

Australia

Antarctica

These two continents are islands.

The South Pole is on Antarctica.

The Seven Continents

Name:

Thursday

Europe

Asia

Africa

Africa is the second-largest continent.

Asia is the largest and most populated.

Name: _____

The Continents

Word Box

Australia   Antarctica
Asia   Africa
Europe   North America
        South America

Write the name of each continent on the correct line.
Then answer the questions below.

1. _____
2. _____
3. _____
4. _____
5. _____
6. _____
7. _____

Which continents have you visited? _____

On which continent do you live? _____

What continents are your nearest neighbors? _____

The Weather

Name:

Monday

windy rainy

sunny snowy

cloudy foggy

breezy drippy

A weatherman gives a weather report.

The Weather

Name:

Tuesday

weatherman

meteorologist

A weatherman is a meteorologist.

When you give a forecast, you predict.

Name:

Wednesday

Humidity

Temperature

is moisture in the air.

tells how hot or cold it is.

When both are low, it's cool and dry.

Name:

Thursday

barometer

thermometer

A barometer measures air pressure.

A thermometer measures temperature.

25

Name: _____

Extreme Weather

Sometimes weather can be extreme. A blizzard is a bad snowstorm. Hurricanes, tornadoes, and cyclones are violent windstorms. A tsunami is a great sea wave. When water overflows and covers the land, it is called a flood.

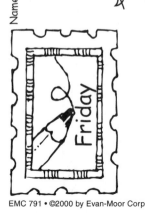
Friday

Copy the paragraph.

Our Presidents

Name:

Monday

George Washington

Washington was the first president.

He was a general in the army.

Our Presidents

Name:

Tuesday

Thomas Jefferson

Jefferson could speak five languages. He

wrote the Declaration of Independence.

Name:

Wednesday

Abraham Lincoln

Lincoln was a Civil War president.

He signed a paper that freed slaves.

Name:

Thursday

John F. Kennedy

Kennedy founded the Peace Corps.

He was assassinated in Dallas, Texas.

Name: _____

Presidential Oath of Office

Friday

I do solemnly swear that I will faithfully execute the office of President of the United States, and will, to the best of my ability, preserve, protect, and defend the Constitution of the United States.

Copy the oath.

Games Around the World

Name:

Monday

Tic-Tac-Toe

three-in-a-row

Tic-Tac-Toe has many versions.

Three-in-a-row wins around the world.

Games Around the World

Name:

Tuesday

Three Men's Morris

Three Men's Morris is an old game.

It was played in China in 1400 B.C.

Name:

Wednesday

Seega

Egypt

Ancient Egyptians played Seega.

Players moved markers on a board.

Name:

Thursday

Picaria

Native American

Players take turns placing markers.

They line up three markers to win.

Name: _____

Achi

Central African children draw the Achi game board in the dirt and gather small stones to use as markers. Copy the directions for play. Then try the game.

You Need:
- 2 players
- 8 markers:
  - 4 light-colored
  - 4 dark-colored
- game board

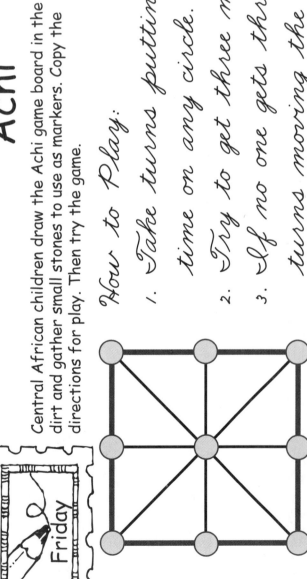

Friday

How to Play:

1. Take turns putting one marker at a time on any circle.

2. Try to get three markers in a row.

3. If no one gets three in a row, take turns moving the markers.

Native American Tribes

Name:

Monday

Onondaga

Seneca

Woodland tribes made homes of wood.

These natives lived by the water.

Native American Tribes

Name:

Tuesday

Pawnee

Sioux

Great Plains tribes tracked buffalo.

Their portable tents were easy to move.

Native American Tribes

Name:

Wednesday

Navaho

Pima

Zuni

These tribes were farmers and artists.

They made rugs, pottery, and jewelry.

Native American Tribes

Name:

Thursday

Kwakiutl

Nootka

These tribes built plank homes.

They held parties called potlatches.

Name: _____

Friday

Native Americans Yesterday and Today

Several million people lived in North
America before Europeans arrived.
Today reservations are located in
thirty-four states. Many Native
Americans live on these reservations.
Other Native Americans live in cities
and towns.

Copy the paragraph.

Name:

Monday

Venus's-flytrap

carnivorous

The Venus's-flytrap eats insects.

Its leaves work like a trap.

Name:

Tuesday

kapok tree

rainforest

The kapok tree can be 200 feet tall.

Many plants and animals live in it.

Name:

Wednesday

saguaro cactus

Sonoran Desert

The saguaro can be 200 years old.

Its skin stores rainwater.

Name:

Thursday

kelp

seaweed

The giant kelp is like a tree.

Its holdfast ties the plant to a rock.

Unusual Plants

Name: _____

Friday

There are many different kinds of plants. Each plant is adapted to the environment where it grows.

The Venus's-flytrap grows in an environment of limited nutrients so it has become carnivorous. The kapok tree has large palmlike leaves. The saguaro cactus has spiny needles. The kelp plant has a holdfast instead of a root.

Copy the paragraph.

Name:

Monday

re

pre

repeat

prevent

unhappy

tricycle

A prefix is at the beginning of a word.

Name:

Tuesday

im

mis

disrespect

misprint

imperfect

ineffective

Add im or un to make an antonym.

Name:

Wednesday

ful

hy

en

ology

hopeful

quickly

wooden

biology

Put a suffix at the end of a word.

Name:

Thursday

less

ment

movement

agreement

hopeless

careless

The suffix less means "without."

Prefixes

re .... means "again"
dis .... means "not"
pre .... means "before"
mis .... means "wrong"

Suffixes

ful .... means "full of"
ly .... means "in a _____ manner"
or and er ..... means "a person who"

disconnected

hopeful

preview

quickly

reorganize

director

misprint

Name: _____

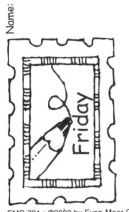

Friday

Copy each word. Write its meaning.

Name:

Monday

spoon

balloon

moon

noon

You seldom see the moon at noon.

Try to pop a balloon with a spoon.

Name:

Tuesday

bug

slug

rug

hug

He is as snug as a bug in a rug.

It would be hard to hug a slug.

42

14 Daily Handwriting Practice

Name:

Wednesday

drink   wrink

think   shrink

Can you drink while you wrink?

Will you shrink? Do you think?

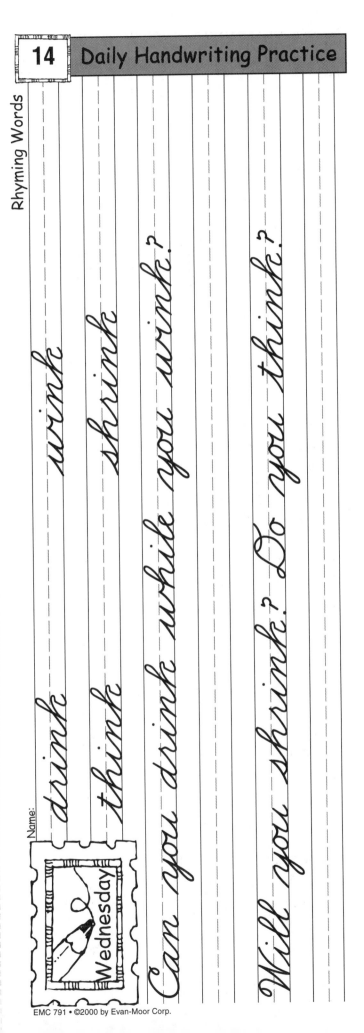

14 Daily Handwriting Practice

Name:

Thursday

freeze   sneeze

trapeze   freeze

When you're on a trapeze,

it's a bad time to sneeze.

Name: _____

Friday

Rhyming Riddles

Answer each riddle
with a rhyming pair.

dinosaur carnivore   *lucky ducky*

redhead   *green bean*

marriage carriage   *flat hat*

big pig

Someone whose hair is the color of a rose

redhead

A large hog

A cap after the elephant sat on it

A vegetable that grows on a vine

A web-footed winner

The wagon used by the bride and groom

A prehistoric creature that eats meat

Rivers of the World

Name:

Monday

Madeira

Purus

Amazon

Japura

Many rivers flow into the Amazon.

They are called tributaries.

Rivers of the World

Name:

Tuesday

Mississippi

Rio Grande

Mackenzie

Colorado

St. Lawrence

The Mississippi is Old Man River.

Name:

Wednesday

Thames

Seine

Volga

Rhine

The Thames flows through London.

The Rhine was important in history.

Name:

Thursday

Yangtze

Tigris

Euphrates

Ganges

The Yangtze is a very long river.

Chinese civilization began along it.

Name: _____

Rivers of the World
Africa

Nile

The Nile is the longest river in the world. The name Nile came from the Greek word "neilos," which means "valley." Water from the river and fertile soil along its banks made this river valley a good place for ancient peoples to live and farm.

Friday

Copy the paragraph.

EMC 791 • ©2000 by Evan-Moor Corp.

Nonsense Rhymes

Name:

Monday

Down by the river,

Down by the sea,

Kitty went fishing with kittens three.

Nonsense Rhymes

Name:

Tuesday

Johnny's over the ocean.

Johnny's over the sea.

Johnny broke a cup and he blamed me.

Name:

Wednesday

Mama, Mama, I am sick.

Send for the doctor,

Quick, quick, quick!

Name:

Thursday

Cinderella dressed in red

Went inside to bake some bread.

How many loaves did Cinderella bake?

Name:

Friday

Nonsense Rhymes Fun

Bubble gum, bubble gum,

chew and blow.

Bubble gum, bubble gum,

scrape your toe.

Bubble gum, bubble gum,

tastes so sweet.

Get that bubble gum off your feet!

Copy the rhyme.

Name:

Monday

silky anteater

howler monkey

The   eats ants.

The   's roar is loud.

Name:

Tuesday

atelopus

gecko

The atelopus is a poisonous frog.

The gecko has suction cups on its feet.

Unusual Animals

Name:

Wednesday

black agouti

crab spider

The agouti cracks nuts with its jaws.

The crab spider looks like a flower.

Unusual Animals

Name:

Thursday

Hercules beetle

toucan

The Hercules beetle is 6 inches long.

The toucan's large beak is not heavy.

Name: _____

Friday

In a Tropical Rainforest

Imagine walking through a rainforest...

Rain drips from the tips of leaves.
Frogs croak and monkeys cry
As giant butterflies quietly pass by.
Imagine standing on the forest floor...
Look up through the understory.
Look past the thick canopy
To the emergent layer and the sky.

Imagine walking through a rainforest...

Copy the poem.

Owls Are Amazing Hunters

Name:

Monday

keen ears

sharp eyes

An owl can see even when it is dark.

An owl can hear animals moving.

Owls Are Amazing Hunters

Name:

Tuesday

sharp talons

hunters

An owl has four talons on each foot.

An owl uses its talons to grab a meal.

Name:

Wednesday

fringed

feathers

The owl has fringed feathers.

The feathers help the owl fly quietly.

Name:

Thursday

no teeth

swallows

An owl tears its food apart.

It even swallows the bones.

Name:

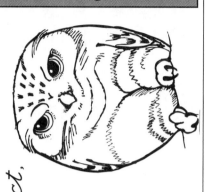

Amazing Hunters

Owls are nocturnal hunters. They catch and eat small rodents. In fact, a single barn owl can eat over one thousand mice in just one year.

Center the title on the first line. Then copy the paragraph.

Whales

Name:

Monday

Whales have blowholes.

The holes are on top of their heads.

Whales use their blowholes to breathe.

Whales

Name:

Tuesday

A whale swims to the surface.

It makes a spout called a blow.

The blow is droplets of water and air.

Whales

Name:

Wednesday

It closes its blowhole and dives.

It can hold its breath underwater.

A whale surfaces, blows, and dives.

Whales

Name:

Thursday

Whales blow differently.

Some whales have one blowhole.

Some whales have two blowholes.

58

Name: _____

Friday

Know Your Blows

The blue whale's blow is narrow and
high. Right whales make two low
blows with their twin blowholes. The
humpback whale has a low blow.
The sperm whale makes a blow that
is angled forward and to the left.

Copy the facts.

The Water Cycle

Name:

Monday

water vapor

invisible gas

Air around us is filled with water.

Hot water changes into water vapor.

The Water Cycle

Name:

Tuesday

breath

warm

droplet

cool

When water vapor cools, it forms drops.

Cold air changes the vapor into droplets.

Name:

Wednesday

liquid

gas

droplets

vapor

Droplets are liquid. Vapor is gas.

Water changes its form over and over.

Name:

Thursday

condensation

evaporation

Condensation = water vapor to droplets.

Evaporation = water droplets to vapor.

Name: _____

The Water Cycle

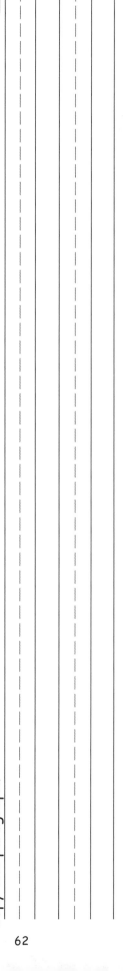

Hot sun warms the Earth. The heat causes water to evaporate. The water vapor rises into the sky and meets cold air. It condenses into droplets. Millions of drops come together to make clouds. When a cloud gets full of water, water drops fall back to Earth.

Friday

Copy the paragraph.

Name:

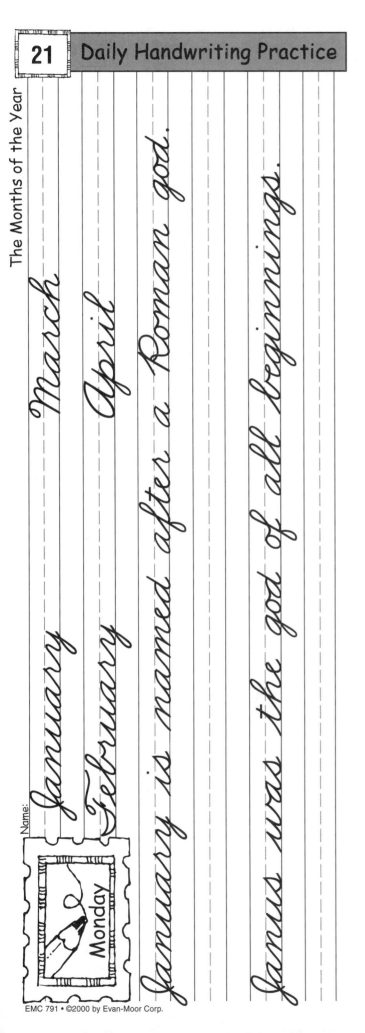

January

February

January is named after a Roman god.

Janus was the god of all beginnings.

March

April

Monday

Name:

May

June

In Canada, Dominion Day is July 1.

U. S. Independence Day is July 4.

July

August

Tuesday

63

The Months of the Year

Name:

Wednesday

September

October

November

December

These names come from Latin words.

The Months of the Year

Name:

Thursday

Winter

Spring

Summer

Autumn

The year is divided into four seasons.

Name: _____

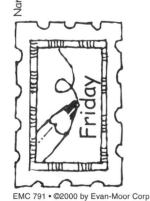

Friday

Months of the Year

Thirty days hath September,

April, June, and November;

All the rest have thirty-one.

Excepting February alone,

And that has twenty-eight days clear

And twenty-nine in each leap year.

Copy this traditional verse.

Using Good Verbs

Name:

Monday

whispered

shouted

The cheerleader "Yea!"

The librarian "Quiet!"

Using Good Verbs

Name:

Tuesday

plodded

crept

The mouse home.

The elephant home.

Name:

Wednesday

dozed

napped

The cuddly kitten

The tired puppy

Name:

Thursday

scribbled

jotted

The man the message.

The child the message.

Name: _____

Poets Use Good Verbs

Copy this portion of the poem *Jump or Jiggle* by Evelyn Beyer.

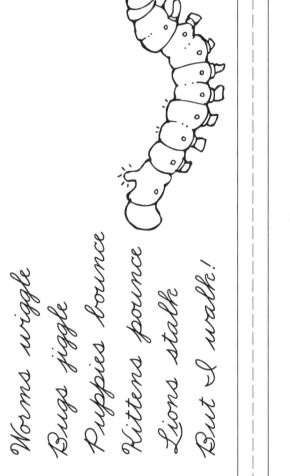

Worms wriggle
Bugs jiggle
Puppies bounce
Kittens pounce
Lions stalk
But I walk!

Friday

Name:

Monday

simile

like

as

A simile uses the words like or as.

The boy ate like a starved animal.

Name:

Tuesday

metaphor

comparison

A metaphor doesn't use like or as.

Her voice was a symphony of sounds.

Name:

Wednesday

personification

human traits

Personification makes things human.

My bike cried as I skidded to a stop.

Name:

Thursday

alliteration

repetition

Alliteration is the repetition of sounds.

Suddenly soapy suds swallowed a sock.

Name: _____

Friday

Copy each example of figurative language by its name.

His voice is as round and strong as a canyon echo.

from *Song and Dance Man* by Karen Ackerman

I could almost see the moon, with a can of paint, spraying the black water.

from *Whale Brother* by Barbara Steiner

Fire is a dragon alive in the night; fiery dragon, glittering bright.

from *Fire* by Shirley Hughes

Peter Piper picked a peck of pickled peppers.

from *Mother Goose*

simile

metaphor

alliteration

personification

Colors and Alliteration

Name:

Monday

red

rose

A riot of red roses rings the rock.

blue blossoms, a blooming blanket

blue

blossom

Colors and Alliteration

Name:

Tuesday

white

whiskers

Which whisker is the white whisker?

Grandpa ground a groove in the grout.

gray

grout

Name:

Wednesday

purple

peacocks

Peacocks paraded in purple plumes.

pink

peony

Pink peony posed for a portrait.

Name:

Thursday

yellow

yolks

Yesterday's yolks were yucky yellow.

green

grass

Greedy groundhogs grab green grass.

Name: _____

Friday

A Cold, Cold Day

On my cold, cold toes are yellow socks.

On my cold, cold hands are blue gloves.

On my cold, cold head is a tall red cap.

On my cold, cold back is a soft tan coat.

On my cold, cold legs are purple sweats.

On my cold, cold nose is an icicle!

Copy the sentences. Then draw and color a picture on the back of the paper.

Name:

Beavers

habitat

Beavers change their habitats.

They block up streams to make ponds.

Monday

Name:

Beavers are good swimmers.

Muscles keep water out of their noses.

See-through eyelids act like goggles.

Tuesday

Learning About Beavers

Name:

Wednesday

lodges

hollow

Beavers build a hollow lodge.

It has an underwater entrance.

Learning About Beavers

Name:

Thursday

Beavers build dams.

They put stones on top of branches.

They scoop mud to fill in the spaces.

Name: _____

Friday

A Beaver's Tale

The beaver's broad tail acts like a rudder to steer when it swims. Its webbed back feet help it swim. Strong front paws help it dig and carry. Two very large orange front teeth gnaw down trees. All in all, the beaver is perfectly equipped to be a pond engineer.

Copy the paragraph.

26 Daily Handwriting Practice

Name:

Monday

Machines

Simple machines

Machines make our work easier.

Simple machines are in all machines.

26 Daily Handwriting Practice

Name:

Tuesday

lever

pulley

A lever is a bar used for lifting.

A pulley makes it easier to move stuff.

Name:

Wednesday

screw

wedge

A screw can move things up and down.

A wedge is used to cut or split things.

Name:

Thursday

wheel and axle

inclined plane

When a wheel turns, the axle turns.

An inclined plane is a tilted surface.

79

Name: _____

Friday

What Is Work?

Write *work* or *not work* below each task.
Remember there must be a force and movement.

work

not work

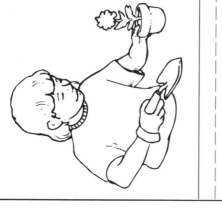

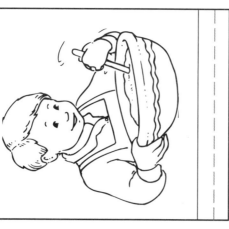

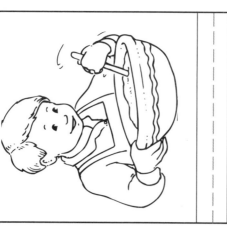

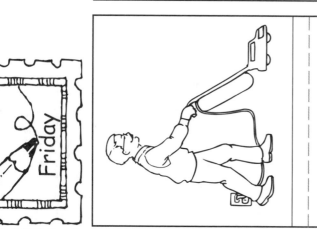

Scientists say that work is done if a push or force is used to move something over a distance. If the thing doesn't move, it is not considered work.

Copy the paragraph.

Famous Quotations

Name:

Listen, my children, and you shall hear
of the midnight ride of Paul Revere.....One
if by land, and two, if by sea.....
"

H. W. Longfellow from *Paul Revere's Ride*

Monday

Famous Quotations

Name:

"I must go down to the seas again, to the
lonely sea and the sky, And all I ask is a
tall ship and a star to steer her by."

John Masefield from *Sea Fever*

Tuesday

Famous Quotations

Name: _____

Wednesday

"They have yarns of a skyscraper so tall that they had to put hinges on the top two stories so to let the moon go by."

Carl Sandberg from *They Have Yarns*

Famous Quotations

Name: _____

Thursday

"Where we walk to school each day Indian children used to play...All about our Native land, where the shops and houses stand."

Annette Wynne from *Indian Children*

Name: _____

Famous Quotations

"Whose woods these are I think I know.
His house is in the village though;
He will not see me stopping here
To watch his woods fill up with snow.....
The woods are lovely, dark and deep
But I have promises to keep,
And miles to go before I sleep....."

Robert Frost from *Stopping By Woods on a Snowy Evening*

Copy the poem.

Name:

Monday

sports

games

physical activity

Kids around the world play sports.

Sports are organized games.

Name:

Tuesday

soccer

football

kick

goal

The most popular sport is soccer.

In most places, soccer is called football.

Sports Around the World

Name:

Wednesday

Malaysia

footbag

Sepak raga is played in Malaysia.

Players pass a footbag to each other.

Sports Around the World

Name:

Thursday

Tennis

France

Tennis probably originated in France.

It was played with a gloved hand.

Name: _____

Friday

The Olympics

The first Olympic Games were held in Olympus, Greece, in 776 B.C. Today's Olympic competitions include many different sports. Approximately 10,200 athletes participated in the 2000 Summer Games in Australia.

Copy the paragraph.

Candy Around the World

Name:

Monday

sugar

candy

sweet tooth

Do you have a sweet tooth?   yes or no

Do you like all kinds of candy?   yes or no

The word *candy* comes from the Arabic word for *sugar*.

EMC 791 • ©2000 by Evan-Moor Corp.

Candy Around the World

Name:

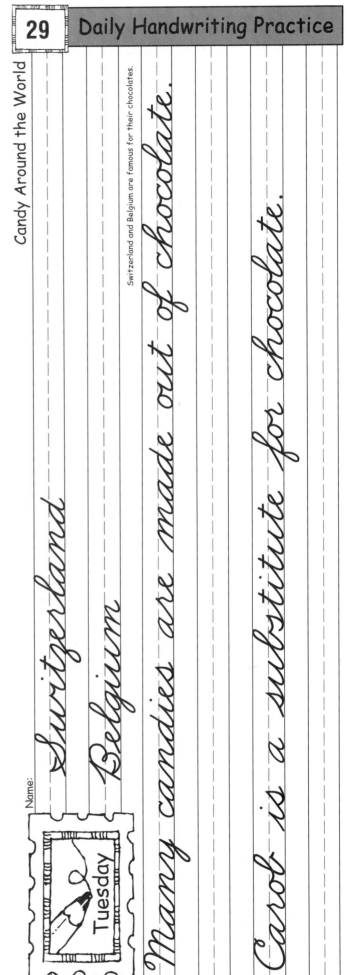

Tuesday

Switzerland

Belgium

Switzerland and Belgium are famous for their chocolates.

Many candies are made out of chocolate.

Carob is a substitute for chocolate.

EMC 791 • ©2000 by Evan-Moor Corp.

29 | Daily Handwriting Practice

Name:

Wednesday

Italy

Middle East

Italian children like cherry nougats.

Middle Eastern children like halvah.

Halvah is a sesame honey candy.

---

29 | Daily Handwriting Practice

Name:

Thursday

Şeker Bayramı

Turkish Delight

Şeker Bayramı is a candy holiday.

It is celebrated in Turkey.

Turkish children like a jellied candy with pistachios called Turkish Delight.

MMMmmm Candy Marbles!!

Friday

Name: _____

What You Need:
1/2 cup chunky peanut butter
1/4 cup evaporated milk
1/4 cup brown sugar
1 teaspoon cinnamon
1 cup crispy chow mein noodles, slightly crushed
1 cup stick pretzels, slightly crushed
1/2 cup chopped nuts

What You Do:

1. Stir the peanut butter, evaporated milk, brown sugar, and cinnamon together. Cook for five minutes.

2. Stir in noodles, pretzels, and nuts.

3. Drop spoonfuls onto a cookie sheet.

4. Chill for one hour.

5. Pop one in your mouth!

Copy the steps for making Candy Marbles.

Learning About Kenya

Name:

Monday

Africa

Kenya

equator

Kenya is on the east coast of Africa.

Kenya lies across the equator.

Learning About Kenya

Name:

Tuesday

Nairobi

Swahili

Nairobi is the capital city of Kenya.

The people speak Swahili or English.

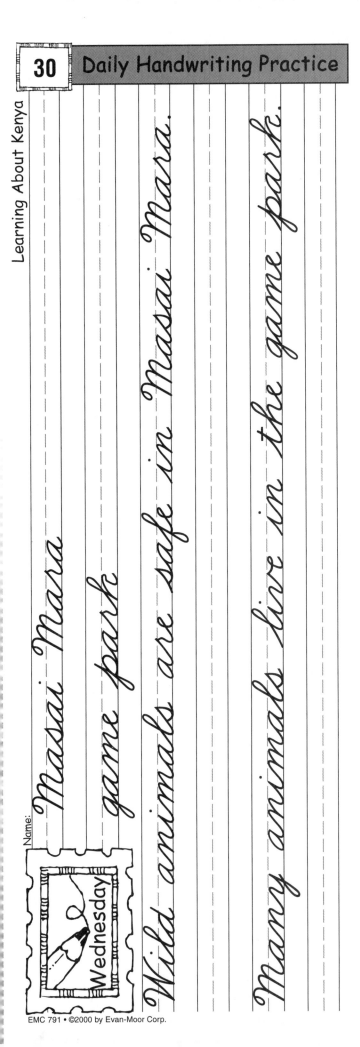

30 Daily Handwriting Practice

Name:

Wednesday

Masai Mara

game park

Wild animals are safe in Masai Mara.

Many animals live in the game park.

EMC 791 • ©2000 by Evan-Moor Corp.

30 Daily Handwriting Practice

Name:

Thursday

Mombasa

harbor

Kenya's second-largest city is Mombasa.

Mombasa has a very busy harbor.

91

EMC 791 • ©2000 by Evan-Moor Corp.

Name: _____

Friday

Kenya's Flag

The flag of Kenya has three stripes on it. The top stripe is black. The center stripe is red and the bottom stripe is green. The red stripe in the center is edged in white. In the middle of the flag there is a Masai warrior's shield with two crossed spears.

The black on the flag represents the people of Kenya. The red represents the blood shed in Kenya's fight for independence. The green represents the fertility of the land. The white represents peace. The shield of the warrior represents Kenya's pride and tradition.

Copy the paragraph.

31 Daily Handwriting Practice

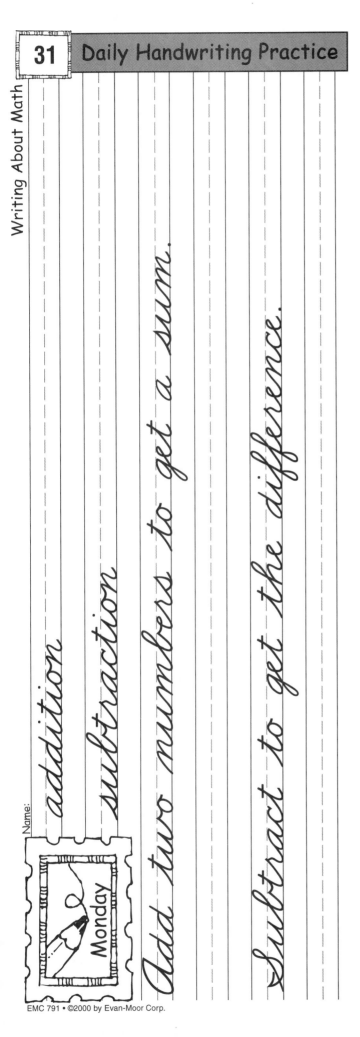

Name:

Monday

addition

subtraction

Add two numbers to get a sum.

Subtract to get the difference.

Name:

Tuesday

multiplication

division

Multiply to get the product.

Divide to find the quotient.

31 Daily Handwriting Practice

Wednesday

Mathematics

Arithmetic

Mathematics is the science of numbers.

Arithmetic is part of mathematics.

31 Daily Handwriting Practice

Thursday

geometry

algebra

There are different kinds of math.

What kind is your favorite?

Name: _____

Friday

Study of Shapes

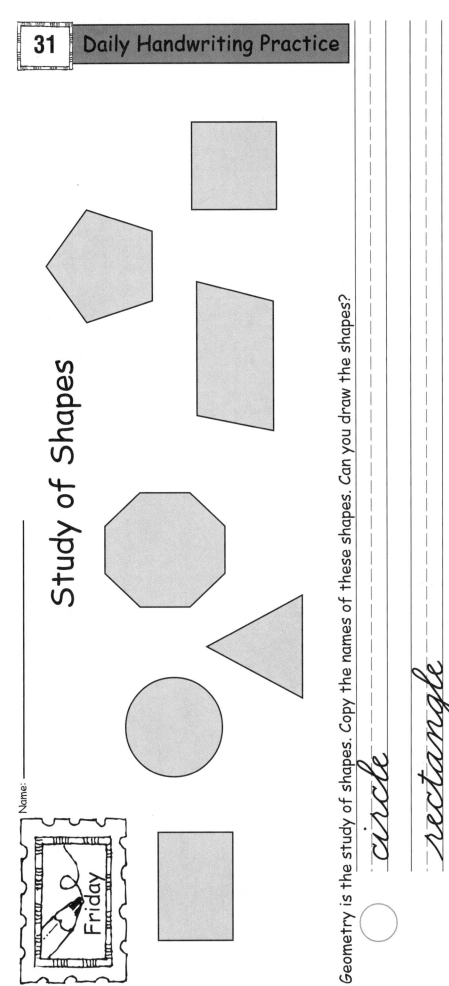

Geometry is the study of shapes. Copy the names of these shapes. Can you draw the shapes?

circle

rectangle

triangle

square

parallelogram

octagon

pentagon

Alphabets Around the World

Name:

Monday

alphabet

Roman

The Roman alphabet has 26 letters.

Alphabet letters represent sounds.

Alphabets Around the World

Name:

Tuesday

Chinese writing uses characters.

Characters stand for words and ideas.

Today Chinese students learn pin-yin.

In pin-yin Roman letters represent Chinese sounds.

Name:

Wednesday

There are different alphabets.

The Arabic alphabet is used in Egypt.

It's used to write Arabic and Kurdish.

Name:

Thursday

Thai alphabet

Asia

It has symbols for different vowels.

It is used throughout Asia.

Name: _____

Hooray for Cyril and Methodius!

Friday

In the late ninth century, two Greek brothers named Cyril and Methodius revised and refined the Greek alphabet. The alphabet was a great success. Today it is called the Cyrillic alphabet. It is used to write Bulgarian, Russian, and a number of other Slavic languages.

Copy the paragraph.

Name:

Monday

A a

A is for ants

amazing, ambitious, architect ants

An adventurous ant ambles annoyingly.

Name:

Tuesday

B b

B is for bumblebee

beautiful, busy, buzzing bumblebee

The bumblebee is by the berry bush.

Name:

Wednesday

Cc

C is for crickets

cheerful, chirping cricket chorus

Crickets, creep up. Commence chirping.

Name:

Thursday

Dd

D is for damselfly

dainty, demure, darting damselfly

Don't disturb the delicate damselfly.

Name:

Friday

E e

E is for earwig

enormous, exotic, excitable earwig

The earwig excavates an earthen nest.

F f

F is for fleas

formidable, flourishing fleas

Fumigate a fast-growing family of fleas.

Buggy Alphabet

Name:

Monday

Gg

G is for grasshoppers

great, gravity-defying grasshoppers

Green grasshoppers gracefully glide.

Buggy Alphabet

Name:

Tuesday

Hh

H is for housefly

hovering, hungry, harassing housefly

Hurry, help me hit that housefly!

Name:

Wednesday

I i   I is for inchworm

itty-bitty, industrious inchworm

Imagine inching innocently forward.

Name:

Thursday

J j   J is for June beetle

just a jet-setting June beetle

June beetle journeys on jaunty wings.

Buggy Alphabet

Name:

K k

K is for katydid

kind, kinetic katydid

Katydid keeps on keys as it sings.

Friday

Buggy Alphabet

L l

L is for ladybug

lovely, little ladybug

Ladybug lifts its wings and launches.

Name:

Monday

M m   M is for mosquitoes

maddening, marauding mosquitoes

Mash the menacing mob of mosquitoes.

Name:

Tuesday

N n   N is for nightcrawlers

ninety nocturnal nightcrawlers

Nightcrawlers never nap as they nibble.

Buggy Alphabet

Name:

Wednesday

Oo O is for oriental cockroach

overbold, objectionable cockroach

Oriental cockroach outruns homeowners.

Buggy Alphabet

Name:

Thursday

Pp P is for praying mantis

peculiar, patient praying mantis

Praying mantis poses on its perch.

Name:

Qq

Q is for queen termite

quiet, quivering queen termite

Quickly the queen lays eggs.

Friday

Rr

R is for rhinoceros beetle

really robust rhinoceros beetle

Regardless of rain, it rambles.

Name:

Monday

Ss

S is for scorpion

scary, stinging, scurrying scorpion

Some scorpions sting striding strangers.

Name:

Tuesday

Tt

T is for ticks

tailless, troublesome ticks

Ticks target tempting, tasty tourists.

Name:

Wednesday

U u U is for underwing moth

unique, unusual underwing moth

Usually the underwing uses its wings.

Name:

Thursday

V v V is for velvet ants

very vulnerable velvet ants

Velvet ants rely on their velveteen coats.

Velvet ants are really flightless female digger wasps.

Name:

Friday

Ww W is for water strider

water-skiing water strider

Its widespread legs walk on water.

Xx X is for xylophanes tersa

excellent sphinx moth

Xylophanes tersa is a sphinx moth.

Name:

Y y y

Y is for yellow jacket

Friday

Yikes! It's a yellow jacket.

Yellow jackets think you are yummy.

Z z z

Z is for zebra swallowtail

Zipping, zooming zebra swallowtail

Zebra swallowtails zigzag with zeal.

112

The Buggy Alphabet Book

by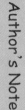

Author's Note

The *Buggy Alphabet Book* represents my best cursive handwriting. I have practiced writing all the letters of the alphabet in lots of different words.

I dedicate this book to _____ .

signature _____

date _____